# SELECTING WORSHIP SONGS

## A Guide for Leaders

Constance M. Cherry

Mary M. Brown

Christopher T. Bounds

TRIANGLE PUBLISHING

*Selecting Worship Songs: A Guide for Leaders*
Constance M. Cherry
Mary M. Brown
Christopher T. Bounds

Direct correspondence and permission requests to one of the following:

Triangle Publishing
Indiana Wesleyan University
1900 W. 50th Street
Marion, Indiana 46953

Website: www.trianglepublishing.com
e-mail: info@trianglepublishing.com

ISBN: 978-1-931283-42-7

Graphic Design: Lyn Rayn
Cover Photography: Cody Rayn
Special thanks to John Maher for engraving the music.

Printed in the United States of America

# CONTENTS

# 1

# INTRODUCTION

The Christian faith is a sung faith. We have embraced the heritage of song from our Jewish forebears, so singing has always been a predominant part of Christian worship. Christians today are still inspired, instructed, spiritually delighted, and strengthened by *corporate* song—the people of God offering their praises and prayers together with one voice.

More options for worship songs are available to church leaders today than ever before. The second half of the twentieth century has yielded a remarkable number of new hymns that have made their way into recent collections. In addition, modern worship songs are written daily, many of them accessible immediately through the Internet. Add to this the proliferation of new songs in every style including Christian alternative, urban gospel, global, responsorial service music, Taizé, psalm settings, and rock. How are worship planners to select what their congregations will sing? How will they choose congregational songs that encourage real worship—that foster participation, understanding, imagination, reverence, lament, thanksgiving, or joy? What makes any worship song worthy of consideration?

Questions like these have prompted us to create an evaluative instrument, a rubric, to help worship leaders in choosing worthy and appropriate songs for local congregations. We gathered ourselves as a theologian, a writer, and a musician—all of us Christian, all of us professors, two of us pastors—to discuss the problem of evaluating congregational songs and to create a useful and discriminating tool for worship planners.

We value many types of worship song, believing that God appreciates variety in voice and personality among congregations. Our focus is not on *type*, but on *quality*. We know that God encourages and blesses whatever is "excellent," "lovely," and "praiseworthy" (Phil. 4:8, NIV). We want to help leaders discern which songs among all types are worthy and beneficial for corporate worship. Perhaps peace could be achieved in some of the current "worship wars" if we were introduced to unfamiliar song types through their best examples. In his book *The Christian, the Arts, and Truth*, Frank E. Gaebelein calls Christians to teach aesthetic discrimination. He contends that it is time for Christians to "outgrow their careless unconcern for aesthetic values and to develop critical standards that will enable them to distinguish good from bad in the art that surrounds them."[1] But exactly what is good and bad in congregational song? What is excellent, lovely, and praiseworthy? What constitutes a strong congregational song—one that inspires and enlivens worship?

The idea of *song* requires two primary elements: music and language. A song is the marriage of melody and words. From that marriage, meaning can be born—something not only or necessarily logical or clinical, but something profound and possibly mysterious as well. When we talk about a *worship* song, of course, we strive for meaning that embodies truth—for expression that comes as close as we can get to *God's* truth, to what we have tried to articulate in the struggles and details of the theology we embrace. In the best congregational songs, good music cooperates with carefully crafted language, works through beauty to express right theology, yielding something of what we know of the glory of the Triune God.

We acknowledge that not all worship leaders see the need to consider seriously the quality of theology, words, or music, when choosing songs for worship. Indeed, many would

Note
_____
[1] Frank E. Gaebelein, *The Christian, the Arts, and Truth* (Portland, OR: Multnomah, 1985), 88.

resist the idea of evaluating any "Christian" song. This became painfully clear in a recent discussion we had with a group of pastors and musicians who lead worship. These worship leaders expressed sentiments such as these: If a song has a Christian message, isn't that good enough? If God gives me a song, who am I not to include it in worship? I was converted while singing a song that was deficient in its theology, but it brought me to Christ; if it works, I see no problem with singing it.

Though such resistance prevails among some, we know that many dedicated pastors and worship leaders think deeply and pray sincerely over each song choice. We hear from many who wonder how they can fairly assess the appropriateness of any given worship song. Our rubric is for them.

Though we do not pretend to be the ultimate arbiters of quality, we believe that our collaboration will serve to help those who struggle to establish standards for their choices. We have no illusion that this rubric is perfect or that it will provide correct answers. In fact, there are no correct answers. The beauty of the rubric is that it will lead to various answers to the question at hand: which songs are most appropriate for any specific church? The same rubric can be used by different kinds of worship leaders, accommodating variables of Christian theology, taste, experience, and education.

Our hope for worship leaders is that at least two things will happen: we will all deepen our thoughtfulness in choosing congregational songs, and we will have a greater assurance of accountability before God and others as to what is voiced corporately in worship.

Our tool was designed to help leaders evaluate how well songs integrate theology, language, and music to express God's glory. We do not mean to reduce worship songs to what is only quantifiable and objective, but desire to help equip those who are entrusted with choosing congregational songs with practical criteria and a workable, negotiable instrument. And while we are enthusiastic about the advance of global worship music around the world, our rubric works best for music with Euro-American roots.

The full rubric is printed in the appendix. We suggest you skim the instrument before reading the following chapters. Sections of the instrument are presented in the body of this text, along with explanatory commentary. The rubric is based on an analytical point system; the sum of the points "earned" by all aspects of a song—its theological content, its lyrical effectiveness, its musical quality—suggests its viability and value as a congregational song in a particular context. Each of the three of us authors worked on criteria of discernment in our own area (theology, language, or music), recognizing the points of overlap and the ultimate need for an overarching integrity in our system. We explained our criteria to one another, a process that prompted valuable discussion.

We unanimously agreed that of the three areas under consideration, theology should carry the most weight. This reflects our strong belief that worship songs should both express and teach the work, wonder, and truth of God. We eventually agreed that theological considerations would comprise half the possible numerical total (30 of 60 points), equal to that of language and music combined (30 points). We also agreed to consider half points in any category, a practice especially needed when several people are involved in the evaluation process.

Using the rubric is simple (though the discussion could prove to be challenging!). Each of the three areas under consideration—theology, language, and music—is broken into five evaluative categories. Simply award points in five categories for each of the three areas. Each theological category can earn a maximum score of 6 points (5 categories at 6 points each = 30 points). Each lyrical category can earn a maximum score of 3 points (5 categories at 3 points each = 15). Each musical category also can earn a maximum of 3 points (5 categories at 3 points each = 15 points). Total the points in all fifteen categories to thereby determine if the song has functional value for your worship setting.

We encourage each group of leaders to decide upon the break point that would disqualify any song under consideration. Our team agreed upon 35 points as an absolute minimum for acceptability; any song receiving fewer than 35 points would not be used in worship in our context.[2] Perhaps your numerical standard would be higher. This provides one more way in which our rubric is flexible and context-sensitive.

We believe that ideally the song evaluation process in any community should be collaborative, the worship leader encouraging conversation and help from those in the congregation with knowledge and understanding of any or all of the three areas. But we realize that in the real world such discussion and collaborative evaluation can't always happen. For the worship leader who must work alone, we hope the following explanation of the criteria on the rubric will prove to be especially helpful.

Despite the use of numbers in a grid, we are ultimately calling for a pastoral approach to song choices for worship. We will elaborate on this in our conclusion; for now, suffice it to say that though this rubric may appear inflexible and constraining, the mature leader will understand that more comes into play than what appears in the rubric itself. This rubric must be in the hands of those who are called, committed, prayerful, and deeply connected to the people within their congregation. Then, and only then, will the spirit of the rubric outweigh its mechanics, and wisdom will prevail.

Note
_____

[2] In our view, a score lower than 35 would suggest too little consideration of theology.

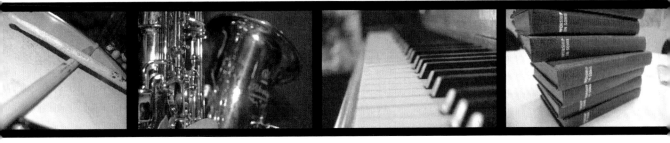

# 2

# THEOLOGICAL CONSIDERATIONS

**W**e express our theology through the texts of our worship songs; those texts, in turn, continue to shape our theology. We learn what we sing; what we express, we come to believe. So it is crucial that our song texts are biblically and theologically sound. Strong congregational songs reinforce orthodox Christian teaching. No matter how creatively arranged or artistically pleasing, a song that misappropriates biblical teaching is inappropriate for Christian worship. On the other hand, perhaps nothing internalizes theology and integrates it with faith as well as song does. We suggest that the theology of any song text be evaluated on the basis of criteria in five categories as shown in the far-left column of the theological rubric: (1) theological integrity according to the song type, (2) biblical allusion or story, (3) Trinitarian ethos, (4) references to God, and (5) corporate or individual expression. We'll consider these five categories in turn.

## Theological Integrity According to Song Type

To consider the theological integrity of any congregational song, the worship leader must first determine the type of song being examined. *The integrity of each song should be evaluated within the context of the song's liturgical purpose.* Most song texts in Christian worship function in one or more of the following ways: (a) as proclamation, which provides instruction; (b) as petition: prayer that requests God's presence, blessing, or divine intervention for ourselves or others; (c) as praise, which exalts God's grandeur or glory and expresses thanksgiving; (d) as exhortation, which edifies worshipers; (e) as a call to action, which invites a congregational response, corporately or individually.

Our rubric acknowledges the importance of understanding the role that each song performs in the context of the service. Before evaluating the theological integrity of a song, the worship leader must first determine the song's purpose. Here it is important to note that a given song does not necessarily need to be eliminated on the basis of undeveloped theology alone. Again, look to its purpose and assess the need for theological depth based upon that. For example, the spiritual "Were You There When They Crucified My Lord?" does not develop a theological idea in-depth, but it does serve the purpose of calling the congregation to meditate upon the death of our Lord.

The category of theological integrity according to song type can earn a total of only 6 points. You'll want to choose one of the five liturgical functions (proclamation, petition, praise, exhortation, call to action) to rate on a scale of 0 to 6.

## Proclamation

A song whose purpose is proclamation functions primarily to communicate the Word of God. Such songs focus on theological themes (one or more) and illuminate those themes (e.g., revelation, the nature and attributes of God, creation, providence, sin, salvation, resurrection). A text that proclaims should be evaluated on the basis of the level of clarity and effectiveness it achieves in announcing truth.

With songs that were written primarily to proclaim central truths about God and faith, two further considerations emerge. Is the text dealing with doctrinal *essentials* or doctrinal *differences?* Certain doctrines are essential to Christianity and must not accommodate variance in interpretation or application. These doctrines include the nonnegotiable teachings of Christianity, beliefs without which Christianity collapses—teachings such as the bodily resurrection of Christ, the Incarnation, the full divinity of Christ, the Trinity, as well as universally agreed upon practices such as love of neighbor, forgiveness, humility, service, and faithfulness. Worship leaders must work to reinforce these essential truths by including a steady diet of them in the worship life of the congregation.

But not all doctrine is equal. Some biblical and theological ideas are distinctive to particular Christian groups, beliefs that arise from different interpretations of Scripture. Variations on beliefs can be biblically sound and held in sincere disagreement. They are important, but they are not at the core of Christianity. Examples include doctrines about predestination, eternal security, infant baptism, Communion, and pacifism. Recently some churches and denominations have moved away from song lyrics that clearly express and emphasize their doctrinal differences. But such songs can play an important role in reflecting the beliefs and heritage of a congregation. We encourage worship leaders to note the distinctive beliefs of their particular churches and consider whether a worship song reinforces the doctrinal differences valued by their churches. In the overall planning of worship, however, song texts expressing doctrinal differences and opinions should be secondary to those expressing doctrinal essentials.

As an example of a song that emphasizes doctrinal differences, we note that the popular contemporary hymn "In Christ Alone" alludes to the doctrines of predestination and eternal security (shown in italics below).

## Theological Considerations: Example 1

No guilt in life, no fear in death,
This is the power of Christ in me.
*From life's first cry to final breath,*
*Jesus commands my destiny.*
*No power of hell, no scheme of man*
*Can ever pluck me from his hand*
Till he returns or calls me home;
Here in the power of Christ I'll stand!

Doctrinal differences such as those suggested in this passage are faithful to some churches' interpretation of Scripture but are not theological views held by all Christian traditions. The point is to note and judge the lyrics of congregational songs to discern what may or may not be appropriate for your worshiping body.

Toward the left of the rubric are four criteria that would qualify a song for a high-ranking 6 points. Such songs strongly address at least one theological idea. They clearly provide instruction to the congregation. The texts provide insight into the teaching, moving beyond the mere statement of the truth to its development. The songs not only set forth a biblical teaching; they also lay out an expectation for worshipers to respond in some way to the proclamation of the doctrine addressed. The hymn "Sing Praise to the Father" proclaims the Triune nature of God and then, in light of this proclamation, calls upon the singer to "Bless the Lord, O my soul."

## Theological Considerations: Example 2

Sing praise to the Father, Creator and King,
whose mercy has taught us a new song to sing;
who made us, and loved us tho' rebels and lost,
and planned our redemption at infinite cost.

(Refrain)
Bless the Lord, bless the Lord, bless the Lord, O my soul,
for the grace that redeems, for the love that makes whole;
O come and adore him, his glories proclaim,
And worship before him—the Lord is his name!

Sing praise to the Savior, Redeemer and Friend,
for grace past all telling, for love without end;
who stripped off his glory, put on mortal sin,
and died in our stead, full atonement to win.

Sing praise to the Spirit, the gift of God's love,
who quickens our hearts with new life from above,
who woos us, subdues us, and seals us his own,
and faultless presents us before the White Throne.

Sing praise to the Father, sing praise to the Son,

sing praise to the Spirit, great God Three in One;

the God of salvation, of glory, of grace,

who wrought our redemption—my soul, sing his praise!

The hymn "The Church's One Foundation" is an excellent example that meets all the qualifications for being top rated in the theological category of proclamation. This stanza (sung as the last, referring to the church as "she") articulates the doctrine of the communion of saints, addressing how the present church has a relationship with the Triune God and fellowship with the saints who already rest with God.

## Theological Considerations: Example 3

Yet she on earth hath union
with God, the Three in One,
and mystic sweet communion
with those whose rest is won.
O happy ones, and holy!
Lord, give us grace that we
like them, the meek and lowly,
on high may dwell with thee.

At the right side of the rubric are criteria for song texts contrary to doctrinal essentials or those that call into question a central teaching. Such songs should earn no points.

| CATEGORY | 6 points | 4 points | 2 points | 0 points |
|---|---|---|---|---|
| Theological Integrity According to Song Type | (A) PROCLAMATION Expresses doctrinal **essential/distinctive** that:<br>• is faithful to Christian teachings that are central, nonnegotiable to Christianity or to a doctrinal distinctive of a given tradition;<br>• clearly and completely states the teaching;<br>• elaborates upon the teaching;<br>• expects worshiper to respond in specific ways (to praise, change, serve). | (A) PROCLAMATION Expresses doctrinal **essential/distinctive** that:<br>• is faithful to Christian teachings that are central, nonnegotiable to Christianity or to a doctrinal distinctive of a given tradition;<br>• is less clear and/or less completely stated;<br>• elaborates somewhat upon the teaching;<br>• suggests worshiper generally respond. | (A) PROCLAMATION Expresses doctrinal **essential/distinctive** that:<br>• is vague or questionable Christian teaching;<br>• is ambiguous and/or gives passing reference to stated teaching;<br>• offers little elaboration upon the teaching;<br>• may or may not expect worshiper to respond. | (A) PROCLAMATION Expresses doctrinal **essential/distinctive** that:<br>• is unfaithful to Christian teaching;<br>• fails to completely state the teaching;<br>• offers no real elaboration upon the teaching;<br>• expects no direct response from worshiper. |

## Petition

A second type of congregational song is that of petition. Songs that voice petitions to God should also maintain integrity according to their purpose. Though their primary intent may not be doctrinal instruction, they too should reflect or imply sound theology. The best songs petition God by demonstrating biblical patterns and attitudes of prayer. They acknowledge the character of God (e.g., the omnipotence of God); they also express the humility and surrender needed on our part as we practice submission to God's good will.

Questionable songs of petition communicate false teaching concerning prayer (e.g., that God always gives us whatever we request) and fail to reflect a biblical model of prayer (e.g., failing to praise God regardless of the outcome). It would be unwise to choose a congregational song that questioned whether or not God would hear our prayer, or that included an ultimatum to God, or that petitioned for evil upon someone else. The chorus "Then I Will Praise You" suggests that praise is fitting only *after* life's difficult circumstances and the dark times of life have been resolved.

## Theological Considerations: Example 4

You seem so far away, You, and Your light;
Darkness has covered me, thick as the night;
I've lost direction, I can't find my way.
God, bring this night to an end.
Then I will praise You, God, I will praise You.
Then I will praise You, my Savior, again.

"Then I Will Praise You" Written by Robin Mann © 1990. robindormann@ozemail.com.au, www.robinmann.com
Used by permission.

Here singers petition God to bring their night to an end *and as a result* they will *then* praise God. Praise is suggested not in the midst of the darkness or during trying times; rather, the text proposes that praise will occur only after we understand and see our way. This is in direct contrast to the pattern of the biblical laments, where statements of praise and trust occur even though the petitioner does not yet see the resolution.

Compare Example 4 with these stanzas of a chorus from the Taizé community.

## Theological Considerations: Example 5

O Lord, hear my prayer, O Lord, hear my prayer;
when I call, answer me.
O Lord, hear my prayer, O Lord, hear my prayer;
come and listen to me.
The Lord is my song, the Lord is my praise.
All my hope comes from God.
The Lord is my song, the Lord is my praise.
God, the well-spring of life.

"O Lord, hear my prayer" Written by Taizé. Copyright © 1991, Ateliers et Presses de Taizé, Taizé Community, France
GIA Publications, Inc., exclusive North American agent, 7404 S. Mason Ave., Chicago, IL 60638, www.giamusic.com, 800.442.1358
All rights reserved. Used by permission.

This song demonstrates that even while waiting for the Lord to hear and answer our petitions, we will still sing songs of praise while we hope in God.

| CATEGORY | 6 points | 4 points | 2 points | 0 points |
|---|---|---|---|---|
| Theological Integrity According to Song Type | **(B) PETITION** Voices prayerful petitions that: • include sound theological instruction concerning prayer; • are obviously consistent with biblical patterns of prayer. | **(B) PETITION** Voices prayerful petitions that: • allude to theological precepts concerning prayer; • are not inconsistent with biblical models of praying. | **(B) PETITION** Voices prayerful petitions that: • suggest questionable teaching concerning prayer; • suggest no biblical pattern of prayer. | **(B) PETITION** Voices prayerful petitions that: • give false teaching concerning prayer; • reflect a pattern that violates biblical models of praying. |

# Praise

Similarly, praise songs should reflect and express a Christian context and understanding larger than praise for praise's sake. This third type of congregational song has its own theological considerations. Corporate expressions of praise and worship should call the community to praise God by stating or suggesting a deep understanding of God's nature and character. Excellent praise songs connect this praise to the creative, saving, and sustaining actions of God; biblical praise generally exalts God not only for who God is, but also for what God has done. (This, too, is a type of proclamation, but it is less about the elaboration of a doctrinal truth and more about the character of God with the focus upon praise.) A praise song with high integrity (eligible for a high rating in our rubric) will also relate the praise to the appropriate person(s) of the Triune God, demonstrating a theological understanding of the various ministries of Father, Son, and Holy Spirit.

At the other end of the spectrum, when praise is vague or generic and could refer to any god, human being, or creature, the song does not facilitate meaningful corporate worship. If there is no mention to the particular recipient of our praise, no reference to what God has done throughout salvation history including in our own lives, the song receives no points on our theological rubric in the category of praise.

One example of a praise song that is moderate in theological development is "God of Wonders." It not only refers to God as Creator, but it also expands upon what that involves; this, in turn, calls for praise.

## Theological Considerations: Example 6

Lord of all creation

Of water, earth, and sky

Heavens are your tabernacle

Glory to the Lord on high

God of wonders, beyond our galaxy

You are holy, holy

The universe declares your majesty

You are holy, holy

Hallelujah to the Lord of heaven and earth.

Stronger yet is "Let All Creation Bless the Lord," which identifies myriad sources of praise to God and then calls on all people to join in that praise.

## Theological Considerations: Example 7

Let all creation bless the Lord,

till heav'n with praise is ringing.

Sun, moon, and stars, peal out a chord,

stir up the angels' singing.

Sing, wind and rain! Sing, snow and sleet!

Make music, day, night, cold and heat:

exalt the God who made you.

O men and women everywhere,

lift up a hymn of glory;

let all who know God's steadfast care

tell out salvation's story.

No tongue be silent; sing your part,

you humble souls and meek of heart;

exalt the God who made you.

| CATEGORY | 6 points | 4 points | 2 points | 0 points |
|---|---|---|---|---|
| **Theological Integrity According to Song Type** | **(C) PRAISE** Expresses praise to God that: <br> • clearly states true aspects of God's nature and character; <br> • develops a deep understanding of God's nature and character; <br> • connects praise to the creative and saving actions of God; <br> • relates praise to the appropriate economies of the persons of the Godhead. | **(C) PRAISE** Expresses praise to God that: <br> • clearly states true aspects of God's nature and character; <br> • develops some understanding of God's nature and character; <br> • may or may not connect praise to the creative and saving actions of God; <br> • may or may not relate praise to the appropriate economies of the persons of the Godhead. | **(C) PRAISE** Expresses praise to God that: <br> • makes reference to God but without reference to God's nature/character; <br> • does not develop an understanding of God's nature and character; <br> • does not connect praise of God to action(s) of God; <br> • does not relate praise to the appropriate economies of the persons of the Godhead. | **(C) PRAISE** Expresses praise to God that: <br> • is generic and minimal in reference to God; <br> • lacks any theological development concerning God's nature/character; <br> • makes no connection to praise of God and action(s) of God; <br> • does not relate praise to the appropriate persons of the Godhead. |

# Exhortation

Some congregational songs serve as means for exhortation; they encourage and edify the community as it worships. The worship of God is not only vertical (God to people–people to God), but also horizontal (people to people in the presence of God). Twice the apostle Paul instructed the New Testament church to sing to one another (Col. 3:16; Eph. 5:19). Paul suggests that songs can serve a purpose to teach and to admonish. One of the purposes of New Testament song in worship was edification. The word *edify* comes from the Latin word *aedifico*, meaning "to build." One role for congregational song is to build faith, to increase hope, to exhort fellow believers in all matters of discipleship, to urge one another forward in our transformation in Christlikeness. Paul is clear that all worship acts, including song, have one purpose: building up.[3] In this type of song, worshipers primarily address one another rather than God, with the larger purpose of advancing the work of God in the world. Christians are transformed into the likeness of Christ for the sake of God, the Church, and world.

The contemporary hymn "The Servant Song" exhorts believers to care deeply for one another by experiencing the joys and sorrows of life together. The community thereby encourages one another to service, which is central to life in the kingdom of God. In our view this song would be eligible for 6 points.

Note
_____

[3] "What should be done then, my friends? When you come together, each one has a hymn, a lesson, a revelation, a tongue, or an interpretation. Let all things be done for building up" (1 Cor. 14:26 NRSV).

# Theological Considerations: Example 8

Will you let me be your servant, let me be as Christ to you?
Pray that I might have the grace to let you be my servant too.

We are pilgrims on a journey, here together on the road;
We are here to help each other walk the mile and bear the load.

I will hold the Christ-light for you, in the nighttime of your fear;
I will hold my hand out to you, speak the peace you long to hear.

I will weep when you are weeping, when you laugh I'll laugh with you;
I will share your joy and sorrow till we've seen this journey through.

When we sing to God and heaven, we shall find such harmony,
Born of all we've known together of Christ's love and agony.

| CATEGORY | 6 points | 4 points | 2 points | 0 points |
|---|---|---|---|---|
| Theological Integrity According to Song Type | **(D) EXHORTATION** Exhorts worshipers by:<br>• focusing clearly and consistently upon encouragement or edification for the purposes of godliness and successful Christian living;<br>• clearly reflecting the larger purposes of the kingdom rather than personal piety alone. | **(D) EXHORTATION** Exhorts worshipers by:<br>• making an attempt to encourage or edify for the purposes of godliness and successful Christian living; (but)<br>• failing to associate growth in godliness with the larger purposes of the kingdom. | **(D) EXHORTATION** Exhorts worshipers by:<br>• offering vague or little encouragement or exhortation; (but)<br>• failing to associate growth in godliness with the larger purposes of the kingdom. | **(D) EXHORTATION** Makes only a passing attempt to exhort by:<br>• making little or no reference to the purpose for edification; (and)<br>• failing to associate growth in godliness with the larger purposes of the kingdom. |

## Call to Action

Finally, songs that are a call to action, that declare the congregation's intention to respond to the Word (and Sacrament) should also be specific and contextual. An active response song on the highest end of our rubric would declare with specificity what the congregation intends to do, associating that intention with the need for divine assistance and with the larger purposes of the kingdom of God. The texts of such songs will express vows, pledges, intentions to follow Christ in true discipleship and obedience, and to serve God and the world; they will call upon God (the Holy Spirit) to empower worshipers to fulfill their songs of commitment. Call-to-action songs should also communicate an understanding of the larger purposes of the kingdom of God rather than limiting the scope to only that action that benefits us in the here and now. Songs of intent should always include a "so that"—a call whereby the worshiper is challenged to take particular action now *so that* the greater kingdom of God is increased.

Unacceptable is the song that suggests an inappropriate or theologically ambiguous response. For example, if a song suggests allegiance to a particular country or political party, or if it calls for withdrawal from the larger world or even the church, the call to response would be contrary to biblical teaching. In such cases the songs should not be awarded any points in this category.

"Your Servant Comes This Hour," a newer hymn of consecration, is rich with possibilities for action. It clearly appeals for divine help in those actions and values the greater purposes of God.

### Theological Considerations: Example 9

Your servant comes this hour in true humility,
believing in your call, O God, and answering, "Lord, send me."

Your servant kneels in prayer, awaiting from above
the touch which sets their life apart for ministries of love.

Your servant stands this day implanted in the word;
prepared to share the holy truth, proclaim it lamp and sword.

Your servant leaves this place with confidence secure,
and by the Holy Spirit bears the fruit which shall endure.

| CATEGORY | 6 points | 4 points | 2 points | 0 points |
|---|---|---|---|---|
| Theological Integrity According to Song Type | **(E) CALL TO ACTION** **Declares** an intention to respond to Word (and Sacrament) that: <br>• declares explicitly what the singer will do; <br>• clearly associates this intention with the need for divine grace or assistance; <br>• clearly associates the intention with the larger purposes of the kingdom. | **(E) CALL TO ACTION** **Declares** an intention to respond to Word (and Sacrament) that: <br>• declares generally what the singer will do; <br>• indirectly associates this intention with the need for divine grace or assistance; <br>• refers to the larger purposes of the kingdom. | **(E) CALL TO ACTION** **Invites or exhorts** a response to Word (and Sacrament) that: <br>• suggests what worshipers should do; <br>• offers vague or no need for divine grace or assistance; <br>• suggests the larger purposes of the kingdom. | **(E) CALL TO ACTION** **Invites or exhorts** a response to Word (and Sacrament) that: <br>• implies what worshipers could do; <br>• violates a biblical essential or type of response; <br>• does not refer to the larger purposes of the kingdom. |

## Summary

The first of five theological categories focuses on a song's theological integrity according to its type, purpose, or liturgical function. So a worship leader's first analytical task is to determine if the song is *proclamation, petition, praise, exhortation,* or *call to action.* Then the leader can apply the rubric's theological considerations accordingly. Very often a song does not fall exclusively into only one of these five types. In this case, look for its essential, predominant purpose. When you find it, work with that. Again, note that this theological integrity category receives a maximum score of 6 points.

## Biblical Allusion or Story

A worship leader should next consider the degree to which a song uses scriptural allusion, language, or story line. We urge you to consider this theological feature because the Scriptures are the text of the story of God. They are replete from beginning to end with what God has done, how God has spoken, and the way in which humans have responded to God. Who could improve upon the psalms, for instance, in their beauty, pathos, honesty, and universal expression? What better narratives are there than those inspired by God? The strongest songs, those that would be awarded 6 points on our rubric, either narrate a biblical story or are rich in identifiably biblical allusion, imagery, or metaphor. When this is the case, the ideas of Scripture are embraced and owned by the community. In this category, points should be awarded based on the amount of detail in the narrative and the clarity and consistency of the biblical language.

Consider, for instance, the praise song that echoes Psalm 84.

## Theological Considerations: Example 10

How lovely is your dwelling place, O Lord almighty.
For my soul longs and even faints for you.
For here my heart is satisfied within your presence.
I sing beneath the shadow of your wings.

(Refrain)
Better is one day in your courts, better is one day in your house,
better is one day in your courts than thousands elsewhere.

One thing I ask and I would seek: to see your beauty,
To find you in the place your glory dwells.
My heart and flesh cry out for you, the living God.
Your Spirit's water to my soul.
I've tasted and I've seen. Come once again to me.
I will draw near to you.

"How Firm a Foundation" is an excellent example of a standard hymn text rich in biblical language. So tied is the text to Scripture that four of the five stanzas appear in quotation marks. Isaiah 43 is quoted generously in these stanzas of the hymn.

## Theological Considerations: Example 11

"When through the deep waters I call thee to go,
the rivers of woe shall not thee overflow;
for I will be with thee, thy troubles to bless,
and sanctify to thee thy deepest distress.

"When through fiery trials thy pathways shall lie,
my grace, all sufficient, shall be thy supply;
the flame shall not hurt thee; I only design
thy dross to consume, and thy gold to refine."

Conversely, a song that not only fails to use recognizable biblical language or story from Scripture, but actually articulates something opposing in nature to biblical ideals would receive no points. An example of this might be "A Beautiful Collision."

## Theological Considerations: Example 12

The heart breaking makes a sound
I never knew could be
So beautiful and loud
Fury filled and we collide

So courageous until now
Fumbling and scared
So afraid You'll find me out,
Alone here with my doubt

Here it comes, a beautiful collision
Is happening now.
There seems no end to where You begin and there I am now
You and I collide

Something circling inside,
Spaciously you fly
Infinite and wide,
Like the moon and sky
Collide

Here it comes, a beautiful collision
Is happening now.
There seems no end to where you begin and there I am now
You and I, collide
Yeah Yeah Yeah

Here it comes, Here it comes, Here it comes now
Here it comes, Here it comes, Here it comes now
Here it comes, Here it comes, Here it comes now
Collide

## Theological Considerations: Example 12 *cont.*

Here it comes, Here it comes now (You and I)
Here it comes, Here it comes now (You and I)
Here it comes, Here it comes, Here it comes now
Feel it coming on, Feel it coming on now, Here it comes now
Here it comes, Here it comes, Here it comes now

"A Beautiful Collision" Written by David Crowder and Jack Parker. Copyright © 2005 worshiptogether.com Songs (ASCAP) sixsteps Music (ASCAP) Inot music (ASCAP) (adm. at EMICMGPublishing.com). All rights reserved. Used by permission.

This text is devoid of biblical allusion. It's also confusing. The main image—of God and an individual colliding—suggests a relationship where there "is no end to where You (presumably God) begin and where I am now." This is inconsistent with Scripture, which describes the divine-human relationship as an "I-Thou"—a relationship where there is a clear distinction between the immortal God of the universe and mortals, between the Creator and the created.

| CATEGORY | 6 points | 4 points | 2 points | 0 points |
|---|---|---|---|---|
| Biblical Allusion and/or Story | Song is rich in biblical language (biblical allusion, imagery, metaphor) and/or is detailed and complete in biblical narrative. | Song contains some biblical language and/or uses narrative in moderate detail and completeness. | Song uses little or no biblical language and/or attempts to use narrative but with little detail. | Song uses language, allusion, imagery, metaphor, or narrative that is opposing in nature to scriptural ideals. |

## Trinitarian Ethos

At the heart of Christianity is the revelation of God as Triune, one God in three persons. Historic Christianity teaches that there is one God in three co-equal persons – Father, Son, and Holy Spirit. The Father is God, the Son is God, and the Spirit is God. However, the Father is distinguishable from the Son, and the Son is distinguishable from the Spirit. Each divine person has all that properly belongs to the divine nature: eternality, omnipotence, wisdom, goodness, holiness, love, as well as other divine attributes. The persons of the Trinity can be distinguished but not separated. Their distinction is not in nature, for they share one divine nature without separation into parts; rather, their distinction is in relationship with one another: the Father begets the Son and the Father with the Son breathes the Holy Spirit. They are one in nature, three in persons.

The ethos of the Trinity underlies our understanding of God and should permeate our Christian thinking and our worship. This is not to say that every congregational song must explain and delineate the mystery of the three persons of one God. But song texts should reflect and reinforce the truth of the Trinity.

At the same time, to address only one person of the Godhead is not inappropriate if the divine person is accurately associated with the work or ministry ascribed to that person of the Trinity in the Scriptures. There is biblical and historical precedence, for example, to speak of the Holy Spirit's role in assisting the believer in prayer. "Eternal Spirit of the Living Christ" calls upon the Spirit to help us as we pray.

## Theological Considerations: Example 13

Eternal Spirit of the living Christ,
I know not how to ask or what to say;
I only know my need, as deep as life,
and only you can teach me how to pray.

Come, pray in me the prayer I need this day;
help me to see your purpose and your will;
where I have failed, what I have done amiss;
held in forgiving love, let me be still.

Come with the vision and the strength I need
to serve my God, and all humanity;
fulfillment of my life in love outpoured—
my life in you, O Christ, your love in me.

This text centers on the work of the Holy Spirit, yet all divine persons are named (God is to be served; Christ is love outpoured). In our view a congregational song such as this would merit 6 points.

Though rare, it is possible that a congregational song could communicate confusing or even anti-Trinitarian thought. One example is the hymn "Who Comes from God?"

## Theological Considerations: Example 14

Who comes from God, as Word and Breath? Holy Wisdom.
Who holds the keys of life and death? Mighty Wisdom.
Crafter and Creator too, Eldest, she makes all things new;
She ordains what God will do,
Wisest One, Radiant One, welcome, Holy Wisdom.

Whom should we seek with all our heart? Loving Wisdom.
Who once revealed, will not depart? Faithful Wisdom.
Partner, Counselor, Comforter, love has found none lovelier,
Life is gladness lives with her,
Wisest One, Radiant One, welcome, Holy Wisdom.

Of the several theological problems with "Who Comes from God?" the most serious centers on the identity and work of "Wisdom." While working with an Old Testament motif of the personification of wisdom, this hymn confuses the distinction between the eternal Son of God (Word) and the eternal Holy Spirit (Breath) and subsumes them into one person, denying the Trinity. Similarly, the hymn confuses the work of the Spirit and Christ. Wisdom is said to hold the keys of life and death—a work designated for Jesus Christ.[4] Wisdom is also said to be Counselor and Comforter—ministries specifically of the person of the Holy Spirit.[5] Confusion increases when reference to "Eldest" suggests that one person of the Godhead existed before another. Although every worship leader should make his or her own value judgment, we would assign no Trinitarian ethos points to "Who Comes from God?"

| CATEGORY | 6 points | 4 points | 2 points | 0 points |
|---|---|---|---|---|
| Trinitarian Ethos | Recognizes and addresses the Triune nature of God by citing all three of the divine persons—Father, Son, and Holy Spirit—by name, title, or work. | Recognizes and addresses the Triune nature of God by citing one or more of the divine persons—Father, Son, and/or Holy Spirit—by name, title, or work. | Fails to recognize and address any divine person—Father, Son, or Holy Spirit—by name, title, or work. | Denies God's Triune nature by containing anti-Trinitarian thought. (For example, that Father, Son, and Spirit are the same person or that the three persons are separable in nature.) |

Notes
[4] Rev. 1:18.
[5] John 15:25–27.

## References to God

How a song refers to the persons of the Trinity is an important consideration for the worship leader. In our rubric, high theological value (6 points) is placed upon the use of biblical names or titles for God. To address God in the same manner as did the biblical authors is to remain within the Judeo-Christian tradition at its best. There is no shortage of names and titles for God; scriptural titles abound. Songwriters do well to investigate the dozens of possibilities and thereby expand their congregants' view of God. One well-known hymn makes mention of no less than nine strong biblical titles for God: King, Shield, Defender, Ancient of Days, Almighty, Maker, Defender, Redeemer, and Friend.[6] The point, however, is not how many biblical titles appear in a worship song but whether or not a song sustains the biblical view of God.

Many songs used in some churches today do not address any divine person by name, title, or work. Songs that use only pronouns for God are theologically weak, for when God is not named there is confusion as to who is being addressed, leaving room for theological misunderstanding. The popular worship song "Breathe" is an example of this kind of ambiguity. The only entity addressed is "You." Unfortunately, because no word for God is used in the song whatsoever, it is highly questionable to ask worshipers to claim that they are "desperate" and "lost" without "You."

| CATEGORY | 6 points | 4 points | 2 points | 0 points |
|---|---|---|---|---|
| References to God | Predominantly and consistently refers to or addresses God (or persons of God) by biblical names or titles. | Minimally refers to or addresses God (or persons of God) by biblical names or titles. | Makes no reference to biblical names or titles for God. | Uses names or titles for God that are inconsistent with biblical practice. |

## Corporate Ethos

Because our worship song rubric is addressing a song's appropriateness for corporate worship, it is critical to understand the way in which the words of songs contribute to or detract from worship's corporate nature. One of the more obvious ways that worship demonstrates that it is truly congregational is in the use of language that clearly identifies the oneness of the singing community. Words that by their very nature refer to the group help demonstrate the fundamental concept of unified worship. An example is the word *church* when used in reference to gathered believers. In this case, songs such as "Rise Up, O Church of God" and "We Are the Church" use specific words to reinforce the community, voicing

Note
[6] "O Worship the King." Words by Robert Grant, 1883. Copyright – Public Domain.

their praise or petition together. Likewise, plural pronouns reinforce the corporate essence of worship. For example, "We Bring the Sacrifice of Praise" very clearly indicates that our praise is offered as a group, not as aggregate persons offering individual praise.

### Theological Considerations: Example 15

We bring the sacrifice of praise into the house of the Lord.
And we offer up to You the sacrifices of thanksgiving,
And we offer up to You the sacrifices of praise.

It is not always so easy, however, to decide what is clearly corporate. Is a song corporate simply by virtue of its use of plural pronouns? Or is it possible that a song can be a shared expression even if the words *I* and *me* are used? Here we make a distinction between *individual* and *personal*. Personal experiences can be voiced in songs and still be corporate if there is cause to believe that the *I* of the song is universally owned by the worshiping community. The gospel hymn "Because He Lives" makes *I* references, yet there is no doubt that this testimony to the power of Christ's resurrection is a universal statement of belief, one that every believer can affirm.

### Theological Considerations: Example 16

Because He lives,
I can face tomorrow;
because He lives,
all fear is gone;
because I know
He holds the future,
and life is worth the living
just because He Lives.

We see "Amazing Grace," "Precious Lord, Take My Hand," and "Lord, I Want to Be a Christian" as additional examples of songs that use a singular pronoun but yet express common Christian assent.

The worship leader must use caution, however, to avoid overusing songs that rely on singular pronouns and suggest an individual experience of God. For instance, to sing "I'm desperate for you" may not be a statement that will resonate with the congregation; it may not represent the consensus of the community. One popular worship song, "Above All," expresses an extremely individualistic perspective of the Christian experience when it asserts that while Jesus was crucified he "thought of me, above all" (assuming the person crucified is Jesus though no direct reference to God/Christ is made anywhere in the song). We would not give such songs a good rating in the theological category of corporate expression.

| CATEGORY | 6 points | 4 points | 2 points | 0 points |
|---|---|---|---|---|
| **Corporate Ethos** | Uses language for worshipers that explicitly indicates corporate assent/ understanding. | Uses language for worshipers that implicitly assumes a corporate assent/ understanding. | Uses language for worshipers that is a mixture of corporate and individual expression. | Uses language that is highly personal in expression. |

## Theological Summary

Here at the end of this theological discussion we lay out the complete rubric for theological considerations. We suggest that the theology of any song text be evaluated on the basis of criteria in five categories as shown in the far-left column of the theological rubric: (1) theological integrity according to the song type, (2) biblical allusion or story, (3) Trinitarian ethos, (4) references to God, and (5) corporate or individual expression.

| THE WORSHIP SONG RUBRIC: THEOLOGICAL CONSIDERATIONS | | | | |
|---|---|---|---|---|
| **CATEGORY** | **6 points** | **4 points** | **2 points** | **0 points** |
| **Theological Integrity According to Song Type** | **(A) PROCLAMATION** Expresses doctrinal essential/ distinctive that: • is faithful to Christian teachings that are central, nonnegotiable to Christianity or to a doctrinal distinctive of a given tradition; • clearly and completely states the teaching; • elaborates upon the teaching; • expects worshiper to respond in specific ways (to praise, change, serve). | **(A) PROCLAMATION** Expresses doctrinal essential/ distinctive that: • is faithful to Christian teachings that are central, nonnegotiable to Christianity or to a doctrinal distinctive of a given tradition; • is less clear and/or less completely stated; • elaborates somewhat upon the teaching; • suggests worshiper generally respond. | **(A) PROCLAMATION** Expresses doctrinal essential/ distinctive that: • is vague or questionable Christian teaching; • is ambiguous and/or gives passing reference to stated teaching; • offers little elaboration upon the teaching; • may or may not expect worshiper to respond. | **(A) PROCLAMATION** Expresses doctrinal essential/ distinctive that: • is unfaithful to Christian teaching; • fails to completely state the teaching; • offers no real elaboration upon the teaching; • expects no direct response from worshiper. |
| | **(B) PETITION** Voices prayerful petitions that: • include sound theological instruction concerning prayer; • are obviously consistent with biblical patterns of prayer. | **(B) PETITION** Voices prayerful petitions that: • allude to theological precepts concerning prayer; • are not inconsistent with biblical models of praying. | **(B) PETITION** Voices prayerful petitions that: • suggest questionable teaching concerning prayer; • suggest no biblical pattern of prayer. | **(B) PETITION** Voices prayerful petitions that: • give false teaching concerning prayer; • reflect a pattern that violates biblical models of praying. |
| | **(C) PRAISE** Expresses praise to God that: • clearly states true aspects of God's nature and character; • develops a deep understanding of God's nature and character; • connects praise to the creative and saving actions of God; • relates praise to the appropriate economies of the persons of the Godhead. | **(C) PRAISE** Expresses praise to God that: • clearly states true aspects of God's nature and character; • develops some understanding of God's nature and character; • may or may not connect praise to the creative and saving actions of God; • may or may not relate praise to the appropriate economies of the persons of the Godhead. | **(C) PRAISE** Expresses praise to God that: • makes reference to God but without reference to God's nature/character; • does not develop an understanding of God's nature and character; • does not connect praise of God to action(s) of God; • does not relate praise to the appropriate economies of the persons of the Godhead. | **(C) PRAISE** Expresses praise to God that: • is generic and minimal in reference to God; • lacks any theological development concerning God's nature/character; • makes no connection to praise of God and action(s) of God; • does not relate praise to the appropriate persons of the Godhead. |

| THE WORSHIP SONG RUBRIC: THEOLOGICAL CONSIDERATIONS *cont.* | | | | |
|---|---|---|---|---|
| CATEGORY | 6 points | 4 points | 2 points | 0 points |
| Theological Integrity According to Song Type | **(D) EXHORTATION** Exhorts worshipers by: • focusing clearly and consistently upon encouragement or edification for the purposes of godliness and successful Christian living; • clearly reflecting the larger purposes of the kingdom rather than personal piety alone. | **(D) EXHORTATION** Exhorts worshipers by: • making an attempt to encourage or edify for the purposes of godliness and successful Christian living; (but) • failing to associate growth in godliness with the larger purposes of the kingdom. | **(D) EXHORTATION** Exhorts worshipers by: • offering vague or little encouragement or exhortation; (but) • failing to associate growth in godliness with the larger purposes of the kingdom. | **(D) EXHORTATION** Makes only a passing attempt to exhort by: • making little or no reference to the purpose for edification; (and) • failing to associate growth in godliness with the larger purposes of the kingdom. |
| | **(E) CALL TO ACTION** **Declares** an intention to respond to Word (and Sacrament) that: • declares explicitly what the singer will do; • clearly associates this intention with the need for divine grace or assistance; • clearly associates the intention with the larger purposes of the kingdom. | **(E) CALL TO ACTION** **Declares** an intention to respond to Word (and Sacrament) that: • declares generally what the singer will do; • indirectly associates this intention with the need for divine grace or assistance; • refers to the larger purposes of the kingdom. | **(E) CALL TO ACTION** **Invites or exhorts** a response to Word (and Sacrament) that: • suggests what worshipers should do; • offers vague or no need for divine grace or assistance; • suggests the larger purposes of the kingdom. | **(E) CALL TO ACTION** **Invites or exhorts** a response to Word (and Sacrament) that: • implies what worshipers could do; • violates a biblical essential or type of response, • does not refer to the larger purposes of the kingdom. |
| Biblical Allusion and/or Story | Song is rich in biblical language (biblical allusion, imagery, metaphor) and/or is detailed and complete in biblical narrative. | Song contains some biblical language and/or uses narrative in moderate detail and completeness. | Song uses little or no biblical language and/or attempts to use narrative but with little detail. | Song uses language, allusion, imagery, metaphor, or narrative that is opposing in nature to scriptural ideals. |
| Trinitarian Ethos | Recognizes and addresses the Triune nature of God by citing all three of the divine persons—Father, Son, and Holy Spirit—by name, title, or work. | Recognizes and addresses the Triune nature of God by citing one or more of the divine persons—Father, Son, and/or Holy Spirit—by name, title, or work. | Fails to recognize and address any divine person—Father, Son, or Holy Spirit—by name, title, or work. | Denies God's Triune nature by containing anti-Trinitarian thought. (For example, that Father, Son, and Spirit are the same person or that the three persons are separable in nature.) |
| References to God | Predominantly and consistently refers to or addresses God (or persons of God) by biblical names or titles. | Minimally refers to or addresses God (or persons of God) by biblical names or titles. | Makes no reference to biblical names or titles for God. | Uses names or titles for God that are inconsistent with biblical practice. |
| Corporate Ethos | Uses language for worshipers that explicitly indicates corporate assent/ understanding. | Uses language for worshipers that implicitly assumes a corporate assent/ understanding. | Uses language for worshipers that is a mixture of corporate and individual expression. | Uses language that is highly personal in expression. |

# 3

# LYRICAL CONSIDERATIONS

**C**hristians struggle with language. And well we should. The knowledge of salvation has been revealed to us in Scripture, through language; the Gospel of John calls Christ himself *the Word*. We see language as a spiritual vehicle and so recognize the need to cherish language, to be careful with it. Certainly we attempt to pay close attention to the language of the Bible, protecting it and considering it both closely and contextually, fussing over translations, citing it, memorizing it. But we use language otherwise too—for practical and impractical reasons, for good and evil.

The Bible instructs us to be careful in all our language use, but exactly what does that mean? Other than citing Scripture, how do we use language in God-pleasing ways? How can and should language be used in church? To express truth and comfort and thanksgiving and praise, of course, but also perhaps to discover these things—and in its finest use, to encourage or create beauty at the same time. This last is an aesthetic goal—a goal of song lyrics.

How well the use of words and language accomplishes these goals involves aesthetic judgment, but it is also possible to create criteria in the application and development of that judgment. We have arrived at five general categories to examine in evaluating the lyrics of congregational songs: (1) sentence structure/grammar/usage, (2) diction: vocabulary and tone, (3) coherence, (4) euphony/sound, and (5) figurative language. All public language involves communication, so the idea of what is *shared* is central to each of these categories.

As in our discussion of theological considerations, we'll look at these five categories one at a time. Note that for the lyrical considerations, a top-rated category score is 3 points, not 6 as for theological considerations.

## Sentence Structure

In good congregational song lyrics, the writer has considered participant and audience expectations. Meaning is conveyed through the conventions of language, through accepted structures, through sentences (or fragments when appropriate) that facilitate clarity or appropriate ambiguity. The ordering—or the *grammar*—of words is central to meaning. *Structure* contributes as much to the meaning and effectiveness of communication (shared meaning) as does vocabulary. A complex sentence suggests a different relationship between and among ideas than a compound sentence does; a question implies something very different from an exclamation. Similarly, word usage suggests consideration for the expectations of others (fellow and future Christians) and the desire to relate knowledge or understanding clearly. When word usage is not standard, but provincial or substandard, a language bond is broken. When word choice is awkward, meaning is lost or at least slowed.

In the contemporary praise song "Our God Is an Awesome God" many instances of substandard usage ("puttin'," "'em," and "it wasn't for no reason") detract from the intended theme of the song: the majesty of God.

## Lyrical Considerations: Example 1

When He rolls up His sleeves He ain't just puttin' on the ritz,
Our God is an awesome God!
There is thunder in His footsteps and lightning in His fists,
Our God is an awesome God!

The Lord wasn't joking when He kicked 'em out of Eden,
It wasn't for no reason that He shed His blood,
His return is very certain, so you better be believin' that
Our God is an awesome God.

This song would receive a score of 0 in this category.

| CATEGORY | 3 points | 2 points | 1 points | 0 points |
|---|---|---|---|---|
| Sentence Structures/ Grammar/Usage | Lyrics include a variety of standard, well-chosen structures and consistently strong choices in grammar and usage. | Lyrics use standard and well-chosen structures and principles of grammar and usage. | Lyrics include instances of non-standard usage, awkward structures, or weak choices in grammar or usage. | Lyrics repeatedly include non-standard usage and/or awkward structures. |

## Diction: Word Choice and Tone

*Diction*—word choice—similarly contributes to the success or failure of any communication or literary piece. *Vocabulary* should be both fresh and appropriate to the *tone* of the song. Lyrics should demonstrate *economy* of language, the ability of well-chosen words to both pinpoint meaning and suggest the breadth of meaning. Charles Wesley showed remarkable command of diction in writing the hymn "Love Divine, All Loves Excelling."

## Lyrical Considerations: Example 2

Love divine, all loves excelling,
Joy of heaven, to earth come down;
Fix in us thy humble dwelling,
All thy faithful mercies crown!

"Love Divine, All Loves Excelling" Words by Charles Wesley, 1747. Copyright – Public Domain.

Wesley's choice of the word *fix*, for example, was brilliant in its simplicity. Like the word *prepare*, *fix* means to get something ready, but *fix* includes the element of longevity, the suggestion of a prayer that what is prepared will stay put. There is nothing difficult about the word *fix*, nothing unusual or pretentious. But it is profound in this context, loaded, in the way that well-chosen language can be loaded. The choice demonstrates not only a freshness, but also an excellent *economy*.

Words in context also create *tone*, the emotional coloring of a communication. The best song lyrics establish a tone consistent with a particular act of worship: praise, confession, thanksgiving, or invitation, for example. The old spiritual "Were You There When They Crucified My Lord?" establishes an appropriate tone of personal sorrow:

## Lyrical Considerations: Example 3

Were you there when they crucified my Lord?
Were you there when they crucified my Lord?
Oh! Sometimes it causes me to tremble, tremble, tremble.
Were you there when they crucified my Lord?

"Where You There When They Crucified My Lord?" Words by unknown author. Copyright – Public Domain.

On the other hand, a mixed or inappropriate tone can cause aesthetic—even theological—confusion or, worse: offense. If the tone of a song is arrogant, elitist, sexist, or exclusive in any way to anyone, its value is diminished. Certainly all congregational songs should carry a tone of reverence for God and of respect for humankind.

| CATEGORY | 3 points | 2 points | 1 points | 0 points |
|---|---|---|---|---|
| **Diction: Word Choice and Tone** | Lyrics show remarkable use of fresh or traditional language, economy, and fully consistent tone. | Lyrics use fresh or appropriately traditional language, good word choice, economy, and consistency of tone. | Lyrics include instances of cliché, ineffective word choice, wordiness, and/or questionable tone. | Lyrics include frequent use of cliché, inappropriate word choice, wordiness, and/or inappropriate or potentially offensive tone. |

# Coherence

A third component of good lyrics is *coherence:* consistency and connections within and among themes, images, and language. Lyrics should focus our meditation and expression, creating an aesthetic integrity. The connections can be traditional—using the example of the harvest as a centering point for a song of thanksgiving or using varied images of God as light throughout a chorus. They can also be surprising, establishing new connections that are fresh, but theologically sound. Coherence can be achieved through *repetition* of ideas or images (perhaps in refrain), through *parallelism* (grammatical consistency or repetition), or through subtle or overt *transitions*, words or phrases signaling time or space connections (as simple as *when* or *after*) and cause and effect relationships (words such as *if* or *because*). Tone and theme should coincide, the story of the crucifixion told in a confessional, regretful tone, the story of the resurrection in a tone of thanksgiving or celebration. An artistic work (such as a song) should cohere, producing in the singer a sense of wholeness, holiness.

The contemporary hymn "Set Your Troubled Hearts at Rest" establishes coherence through grammatical parallelism (imperative structures) followed by declarative structures within each stanza and repetition.

# Lyrical Considerations: Example 4

Set your troubled hearts at rest,
Set your troubled hearts at rest.
I have stilled the wildest thunder;
I will give you rest.

Lay your heavy burdens down,
Lay your heavy burdens down.
I have come to be your brother;
Lay your heavy burdens down.

Trust me in your unbelief,
Trust me in your unbelief.
I have met you in your doubting;
Trust me and believe.

Set your troubled hearts at rest,
Set your troubled hearts at rest.
I have made a dwelling for you;
I will give you rest.

| CATEGORY | 3 points | 2 points | 1 points | 0 points |
|---|---|---|---|---|
| **Coherence** | Lyrics show remarkable consistency and connections within and between themes and tone; remarkable connections within and among language, ideas, and images. | Lyrics show consistency within and between themes and tone; clear connections within and among language, ideas, and images. | Lyrics include instances of inconsistency in themes and tone; instances of failure to connect ideas and/or language. | Lyrics include frequent inconsistencies in themes and tone; repeated failure to connect ideas and/or language. |

## Euphony/Sound

Because lyrics are expressed orally, the sounds of the language itself are important to the quality of the piece. Tongue twisters have no place in corporate songs, nor do constructions that are in any way difficult to articulate. If the tongue or mouth is in any way tripped, singing will falter or stop. But even if there is no problem with *articulation*, the sounds of the language ought to be as pleasing as the sounds of the music. As a traditional feature of lyrics, *end rhyme* can make or break a song. When it works well, naturally, with the grammar and tone of the lyrics, it produces an aesthetic integrity. When it is forced, included only for the sake of the rhyme itself, or when it is completely predictable, it can detract from the message and beauty of the song. Many accomplished songwriters use off rhyme. This technique does not require both the internal vowel sounds and the end consonant sound to be exactly the same; it simply repeats one or the other. *Love*, for instance, is an off rhyme of *live*, and *cross* and *bliss* are off rhymes. Using these techniques provides much more freedom in language, so that neither truth nor art has to take a back seat to form. When any sound device calls too much attention to itself, both meaning and beauty are lost. Good lyrics are both natural and surprising in their sounds.

The praise chorus "I Want to Be with You" holds few surprises, the two parts of the song both employing end rhyme in a completely predictable way. In our rubric, this chorus would receive a 1 in the euphony/sound category.

### Lyrical Considerations: Example 5

I want to be with You
in the daytime and the nighttime too,
oh Lord, I want to be with You.

You are there in the morning,
ever faithful and true,
I look around and I find You,
all the day through.

| CATEGORY | 3 points | 2 points | 1 points | 0 points |
|---|---|---|---|---|
| Euphony/Sound | Lyrics show remarkable grace and remarkable or surprising use of rhyme and other sound devices. | Lyrics show general grace and effective rhyme and other sound devices. | Lyrics include instances of gracelessness, including difficult-to-articulate words or phrases, flat or awkward sounds, predictable rhyme, and/or ineffective sound devices. | Lyrics include repeated, difficult-to-articulate words and phrases, forced rhyme, repeated awkward sounds, and/or pervasive, ineffective use of sound devices. |

## Figurative Language

Like much of the Bible, good song lyrics make good use of *figurative language*—ideas expressed through nonliteral language. They are like poetry in that way. When the psalmist says "The Lord is my shepherd," we understand that God takes care of us—but we also know and feel much more. Similarly, when we sing "Shine, Jesus, Shine," we speculate on the implications and mystery of the *metaphor* of God as light. Abstract ideas are often best expressed through figurative language, which at its best is specific language, drawing us to something concrete that helps us to understand the abstraction. Emotions are often engaged through *image* (e.g., "whose canopy space," see "O Worship the King," example, below)—that which requires the involvement of the senses. Like all language, however, figurative language may be used poorly—a distraction, or worse, a distortion. When metaphor becomes cliché, we seldom pay attention. When metaphor is mixed, we end up confused. When figurative language is used effectively, however, we are appreciative, involved, and able to hold onto the profound mysteries of our God and of our faith.

We would be hard pressed to find an example of a song that would better demonstrate a 3 in this category than the hymn "O Worship the King."

### Lyrical Considerations: Example 6

O worship the King
all-glorious above;
O gratefully sing
his pow'r and his love,
our Shield and Defender
the Ancient of Days,
pavilioned in splendor
and girded with praise!

## Lyrical Considerations: Example 6 *cont.*

O tell of his might,
O sing of his grace,
whose robe is the light,
whose canopy space!
His chariots of wrath
the deep thunderclouds form,
and dark is his path
on the wings of the storm.

"O Worship the King" Words by Robert Grant, 1833. Copyright – Public Domain.

| CATEGORY | 3 points | 2 points | 1 points | 0 points |
|---|---|---|---|---|
| Figurative Language | Lyrics show remarkable, artful use of figurative language, imagery, and specificity. | Lyrics use imagery and figurative language well; generalization or abstraction is tempered by image or specificity. | Lyrics include instances of cliché, stale imagery or figurative language, or excessive use of generalization or abstraction. | Lyrics are clichéd, use inappropriate figurative language (such as mixed metaphor) and/or pervasive generalization or abstraction. |

## Lyrical Summary

If the lyrics of a worship song are strong, it should earn between 12 and 15 points on this rubric. But how the language interacts with music is essential and how language and music suggest or express good theology is crucial.

Here is the complete rubric for language considerations:

| THE WORSHIP SONG RUBRIC: LYRICAL CONSIDERATIONS | | | | |
| --- | --- | --- | --- | --- |
| CATEGORY | 3 points | 2 points | 1 points | 0 points |
| Sentence Structures/ Grammar/Usage | Lyrics include a variety of standard, well-chosen structures and consistently strong choices in grammar and usage. | Lyrics use standard and well-chosen structures and principles of grammar and usage. | Lyrics include instances of non-standard usage, awkward structures, or weak choices in grammar or usage. | Lyrics repeatedly include non-standard usage and/or awkward structures. |
| Diction: Word Choice and Tone | Lyrics show remarkable use of fresh or traditional language, good word choice, economy, and fully consistent tone. | Lyrics use fresh or appropriately traditional language, good word choice, economy, and consistency of tone. | Lyrics include instances of cliché, ineffective word choice, wordiness, and/or questionable tone. | Lyrics include frequent use of cliché, inappropriate word choice, wordiness, and/or inappropriate or potentially offensive tone. |
| Coherence | Lyrics show remarkable consistency and connections within and between themes and tone; remarkable connections within and among language, ideas, and images. | Lyrics show consistency within and between themes and tone; clear connections within and among language, ideas, and images. | Lyrics include instances of inconsistency in themes and tone; instances of failure to connect ideas and/or language. | Lyrics include frequent inconsistencies in themes and tone; repeated failure to connect ideas and/or language. |
| Euphony/Sound | Lyrics show remarkable grace and remarkable or surprising use of rhyme and other sound devices. | Lyrics show general grace and effective rhyme and other sound devices. | Lyrics include instances of gracelessness, including difficult-to-articulate words or phrases, flat or awkward sounds, predictable rhyme, and/or ineffective sound devices. | Lyrics include repeated, difficult-to-articulate words and phrases, forced rhyme, repeated awkward sounds, and/or pervasive, ineffective use of sound devices. |
| Figurative Language | Lyrics show remarkable, artful use of figurative language, imagery, and specificity. | Lyrics use imagery and figurative language well; generalization or abstraction is tempered by image or specificity. | Lyrics include instances of cliché', stale imagery or figurative language, or excessive use of generalization or abstraction. | Lyrics are clichéd, use inappropriate figurative language (such as mixed metaphor) and/or pervasive generalization or abstraction. |

# 4

# MUSICAL CONSIDERATIONS

Singing requires tunes. Tunes transport the texts of the songs to their destination—either to God, to other worshipers, or even to one's self—depending upon who is being addressed in the song. But are all sacred musical compositions created equal? If the text is good or even adequate, does it really matter what music accompanies it? If one assumes that not all music is created equal, how *does* a worship leader decide upon the adequacy of the music that transports the text? What will be the criteria one uses to render any tune worthy to be sung by the congregation (or not)?

Though music apart from a text is technically neither sacred nor secular,[7] music is not worth singing simply because it accompanies an acceptable religious text. In other words, a tune is not value-free. The worthiness of the music itself should be considered in choosing congregational songs.

Clarification of a few terms may be helpful. *Song* is a lyrical text set to music. Of course, songs are written for any occasion and are not necessarily religious in nature. *Congregational song* refers to any and all types of songs that are written to be sung by the body of Christ when they gather for corporate worship. Congregational songs include hymns, chant, psalms, choruses, and gospel hymns, to name a few common types. *Tune* refers strictly to the melody of the song. Historically, the melodies of hymns have been referred to as "hymn tunes" or simply "tunes."

We suggest that you consider musical features in five categories when you evaluate congregational song for Christian worship: (1) strength of the melody, (2) rhythmic vitality, (3) harmonic support, (4) compatibility of music and text, and (5) suitability for congregational singing.

## Strength of Melody

First, an effective song must have a strong melody. The melody is the tune—the memorable arrangement of musical notes (with corresponding lengths) that gives the tune its identifiable character. Strong melodies are *purposeful* in that they have a point of origination, seem to "travel" somewhere interesting, and conclude at a place of rest or resolution.

Melodies should not generally be static but have plenty of motion. A good melody combines some *step-wise motion* (neighboring notes on a scale) as well as *appropriate leaps* (nonneighboring notes of various distances apart) as it builds toward a climax.

Strong melodies also are sensitive to the *vocal range* of the melodic line. The range of the melody refers to the amount of "musical territory" it covers (the distance from the lowest to the highest notes). Think about where the "action" of the melody lingers. For example, does the melody require the singers to sustain very high pitches for a very long time? If so, is this conducive to the communication of the text? Is the range realistic for the capabilities of the congregation?

Good melodies use *standard compositional devices*; after all, tunes are meant to be sung by groups of singers who will need to comprehend the logic of the melody easily and intuitively. The composer will use devices such as repetition of musical ideas for coherence, creation of arrival points where the melody seems to temporarily rest (cadences), and effective phrasing (creating sub-units of the melody that interpret the various lines of the text).

Note
---
[7] Here we are speaking in the most technical sense. It is true that many instrumental pieces were/are written exclusively for use in religious settings (the J.S. Bach prelude and fugues come to mind). However, in the most basic sense, a musical piece without words can only imply theological or biblical truth.

An excellent melody is able to stand on its own without the text. In other words, it is attractive and interesting in and of itself; it does not need the text in order to have value.

Last, good melodies are memorable—they will stay with you after you have sung them. Poorly written melodies can also be memorable (unfortunately!); nevertheless, a good melody will recur to you after you have sung it.

One example of a fine melody is SLANE,[8] a tune most associated with the hymn "Be Thou My Vision." Notice how the melody's first phrase begins at a moderate pitch, the second phrase starts a little higher, while the third phrase (both musically and lyrically) starts even higher and reaches a peak, only to return to the moderate pitch (as at the beginning) to start the fourth phrase. This gives a sense of progression to the melody overall. There is also a shape to each musical phrase that rises and falls so naturally. Step-wise motion of the notes predominates, but with a nice balance of leaps; the range is highly accessible with an obvious climax at the third line as the notes climb to help add momentum to the tune; the melody arrives at natural places of rest at the end of each musical phrase. This tune is considered by many to be simple and lovely in its own right—so much so that though hundreds of years old, it is being reclaimed by contemporary worshipers. We would award this tune 3 points.

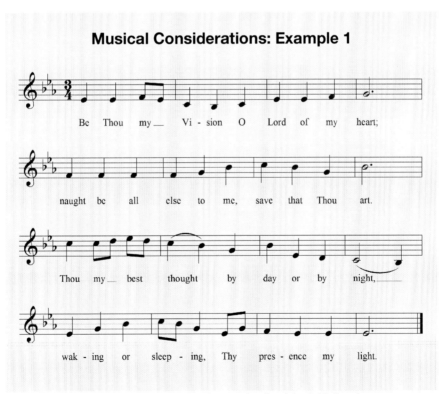

**Musical Considerations: Example 1**

"Be Thou MyVision" Words by unknown author. Copyright – Public Domain
SLANE. By unknown composer. Copyright – Public Domain

Note
___

[8] Most hymn tunes are given a name independent of the text. It is traditional practice to capitalize the names of hymns tunes. SLANE is a traditional Irish melody.

| CATEGORY | 3 points | 2 points | 1 points | 0 points |
|---|---|---|---|---|
| Melody | Melody has direction, uses leaps and steps judiciously, is balanced in vocal range, uses standard melodic features, stands on its own, and is memorable. | Melody has moderate direction, uses a few awkward leaps and steps, rests heavily in one part of the range, and/or is somewhat memorable. | Melody lacks direction, treats leaps and steps awkwardly, is somewhat monotonous, or is not easily remembered. | Melody lacks logic, variety, appeal, and is not memorable. |

## Rhythmic Vitality

A second musical feature to be considered is rhythmic vitality. Rhythm, like the melody, should be *purposeful*; that is, rhythm, too, should "go somewhere." In a song with rhythmic vitality, rhythm helps the melody to push forward or to relax. Good rhythm will *portray the action of the text.* It will also assist in *good declamation* (making sure that the musical accent coincides with the verbal accent). Strong word syllables are matched with strong musical accents in the rhythmic patterns. Last, whatever rhythm is used must be *accessible* to the congregation. In other words, it must not be so bland as to bore them, or so complicated as to be difficult to sing.

An example of rhythmic vitality in a tune is the music that accompanies the contemporary chorus "Let There Be Praise." The frequent use of syncopation drives the melody forward and contributes to the spirited feel of the text; at the same time it is not so complicated for corporate singing. The rhythmic pattern that is established in the beginning is repeated throughout the chorus which makes it quite accessible to the average singer. This tune establishes rhythms which provide interest, support the text, and are relatively easy for any congregation to embrace due to their consistent repetition. The following tune, for "Let There Be Praise," would receive 3 points in our rubric for rhythmic vitality.

# Musical Considerations: Example 2

By contrast, the gospel hymn "O Happy Day" lacks rhythmic vitality; it uses a limited number of rhythmic patterns that become dull and predictable. In our view, this tune would receive 0 in this category.

## Musical Considerations: Example 3

"O Happy Day" Words by Philip Doddridge. Copyright – Public Domain
HAPPY DAY. By unknown composer; refrain attributed to Edward F. Rimbault. Copyright – Public Domain

| CATEGORY | 3 points | 2 points | 1 points | 0 points |
|---|---|---|---|---|
| **Rhythmic Vitality** | Rhythm has direction, is interesting, portrays the action of the text, assists in good declamation, and is reasonable for the singers to master. | Rhythm is of moderate interest; does not add to or detract from the melody and/or text, or has one or more obstacles for the singers. | Rhythm is unnecessarily repetitious, draws attention to itself, is inconsistent in the use of accents with the text, and/or discourages the singers. | Rhythm works against the melody and/or text, defeating the message of the song, or is too difficult to sing. |

## Harmonic Support

The third feature is harmonic support. Harmony is the use of complementary notes, either in the accompaniment or in other voice parts, which enhance the melody. The simultaneous sounding of these auxiliary notes is sometimes referred to as chords. Not all congregational songs presuppose that harmony is necessary. For instance, unison chant has no harmonic support, for the beauty and simplicity of the melodic line is sufficient to accomplish the purposes of the sung liturgy. However, most congregational song today uses harmony. Good harmony *helps the melody progress*; it enriches the melody without covering it up. A good balance of *dissonance* (creating tension within the harmony by combining pitches which may conflict with our sense of peace and/or rest) and *consonance* (combining pitches that seem to release this tension) creates musical interest as well as a sense of pathos. Because congregational song is sung by many voices, good harmonic writing will *lend itself well to the singing of parts* (various voices singing various harmonic lines).

The gospel hymn "O Happy Day" mentioned above as a weak example of rhythmic vitality, also serves as a weak example of harmonic support. There are very few complementary notes used (few chord changes); in fact, some hymnals render this hymn with no more than two chords (other hymnals have tried to embellish the chords to add harmonic interest—unsuccessfully). The harmony for this hymn is very dull and predictable at best and would receive a .5.

| CATEGORY | 3 points | 2 points | 1 points | 0 points |
|---|---|---|---|---|
| **Harmonic Support** | Harmony facilitates the progression of the melody, enriches the melody without covering it, uses helpful amounts of dissonance and consonance, and/or lends itself to singing in parts. | Harmony is somewhat predictable, use of dissonance and/or consonance is questionable, and/or lends itself less to singing in parts. | Harmony is dull and predictable. | Harmony is in conflict with the melody and text. |

## Compatibility of Music and Text

Fourth, a good worship song must have compatibility of music and text. There should be a good union between the message of the text and what the music itself suggests. Both the text and the music have meaning in and of themselves. Yet it is possible to have both a strong text and a strong tune but not have a strong *song* simply because text and tune do not support each other. The best worship songs are those where the two elements come together to form unified meaning(s). Powerful moments in congregational song occur when an excellent text and excellent music combine in full support of the message and purpose of the song.

The music of the song serves the text of the song by helping to interpret the text. To accomplish this, the basic musical features (melody, rhythm, and harmony) aid the text—reinforcing, emphasizing, adorning it—letting the text emerge in its own beauty surrounded by appropriate music. When this occurs, the whole is greater than the sum of its parts; the meaning of the worship song exceeds the meaning of either the text or the music alone.

The contemporary hymn "Here I Am, Lord" is an excellent example of the compatibility of music and text. Note how the melody is emphatic for the stanzas where it is the Lord who is speaking. But when questions are posed, first by the Lord at the end of each stanza ("Whom shall I send?") and then in the refrain where the singer asks, "Is it I, Lord?" the melody also "asks a question" musically by rising in pitch; the direction of the music reinforces the text that is asking a question. In our evaluation "Here I Am, Lord" would receive top ranking in this category of the rubric.

# Musical Considerations: Example 4

| CATEGORY | 3 points | 2 points | 1 points | 0 points |
|---|---|---|---|---|
| **Compatibility of Music and Text** | Musical components contribute significantly in supporting, highlighting, and interpreting the text. | Some but not all of the musical components contribute to the text. | Musical components neither contribute to nor detract from the text; compatibility is neutral. | Some musical components seem to be in conflict with the tenor of the text. |

## Suitable for Corporate Singing

Ultimately, music must be suitable for corporate singing. We must consider the musical capabilities of our congregations. Does a particular song fit the vocal range of your congregation? Are they able to sing the lowest and highest notes of the music without straining? Does the song *use repetition* so that phrases are familiar from stanza to stanza? Is it easily *sung in unison* (all singers on the melody)? Does the music *adapt well to harmonic singing*? Congregations should be taught to sing; they should be encouraged to increase in their singing capabilities. Still, there is a general "window of accessibility" to be considered for the average congregation. Each leader must discern what their congregation's current singing capabilities are while leading them to grow in their singing skills to the glory of God.

The tune commonly used with the hymn "And Can It Be that I Should Gain?" poses some significant challenges for the average congregation to sing today. This is regrettable, for Charles Wesley's text holds great theological merit. The melodic line uses very wide leaps incessantly, thereby seeming quite disjointed throughout; frankly, the melody moves all over the place. The melody also encompasses a very wide range, requiring the congregation to sing a span of three notes beyond an octave. Asking singers to sing both high and low notes frequently in the course of a lengthy hymn places undue demands on them. What's more, the tune does not lend itself to excellent harmonic singing. The alto line is dull; the bass part also incorporates many wide leaps. The refrain is the only part of the hymn that is the exception to the concerns stated here (and, in fact, has some nice features), but it is so brief that it cannot redeem the problems found in the majority of the hymn. This song would receive .5 points in the suitability category.

# Musical Considerations: Example 5

"And Can It Be that I Should Gain?" Words by Charles Wesley. Music by Thomas Campbell. Copyright – Public Domain.

| CATEGORY | 3 points | 2 points | 1 points | 0 points |
|---|---|---|---|---|
| **Suitability for Singing** | Music is accessible for corporate singing in relation to vocal range, structural repetition, and ease of unison and/or singing in parts. | Music includes some hindrances to corporate singing. | Music has significant hindrances to corporate singing in one or more aspects. | Music is too difficult to sing corporately. |

# Musical Summary

Musical considerations are crucial; for while we believe that ultimately the message of a song is of utmost importance, in the end, what a given congregation is able to sing (and embrace as musically meaningful) will allow the chosen text to be of service to the community or not. The best texts still need excellent tunes to deliver them.

| THE WORSHIP SONG RUBRIC: MUSICAL CONSIDERATIONS | | | | |
|---|---|---|---|---|
| **CATEGORY** | **3 points** | **2 points** | **1 points** | **0 points** |
| **Melody** | Melody has direction, uses leaps and steps judiciously, is balanced in vocal range, uses standard melodic features, stands on its own, and is memorable. | Melody has moderate direction, uses a few awkward leaps and steps, rests heavily in one part of the range, and/or is somewhat memorable. | Melody lacks direction, treats leaps and steps awkwardly, is somewhat monotonous, or is not easily remembered. | Melody lacks logic, variety, appeal, and is not memorable. |
| **Rhythmic Vitality** | Rhythm has direction, is interesting, portrays the action of the text, assists in good declamation, and is reasonable for the singers to master. | Rhythm is of moderate interest; does not add to or detract from the melody and/or text, or has one or more obstacles for the singers. | Rhythm is unnecessarily repetitious, draws attention to itself, is inconsistent in the use of accents with the text, and/or discourages the singers. | Rhythm works against the melody and/or text, defeating the message of the song, or is too difficult to sing. |
| **Harmonic Support** | Harmony facilitates the progression of the melody, enriches the melody without covering it, uses helpful amounts of dissonance and consonance, and/or lends itself to singing in parts | Harmony is somewhat predictable, use of dissonance and/or consonance is questionable, and/or lends itself less to singing in parts. | Harmony is dull and predictable. | Harmony is in conflict with the melody and text. |
| **Compatibility of Music and Text** | Musical components contribute significantly in supporting, highlighting, and interpreting the text. | Some but not all of the musical components contribute to the text. | Musical components neither contribute to nor detract from the text; compatibility is neutral. | Some musical components seem to be in conflict with the tenor of the text. |
| **Suitability for Singing** | Music is accessible for corporate singing in relation to vocal range, structural repetition, and ease of unison and/or singing in parts. | Music includes some hindrances to corporate singing. | Music has significant hindrances to corporate singing in one or more aspects. | Music is too difficult to sing corporately. |

# 5

# CONCLUSION

**W**e present this song rubric as a practical and helpful tool in the process of evaluating worship songs. No one is completely objective; that is why we need a means of bringing some objectivity to bear upon our most important tasks as Christian worship leaders. We suggest that you use the rubric flexibly. Let it serve you rather than your serving it.

We hope to see this rubric being used to practice pastoral theology—theology that takes place in community. This will require pastoral musicians and truly pastoral clergy. The word *pastoral* in this context does not consider whether someone is ordained, credentialed, or holds a clerical rank. Rather, to be pastoral is simply to be judicious in how one leads others. To be a pastoral worship leader, one must listen to God, for God *will* direct us all as we seek to be faithful in the song selection process. In this sense, the pastoral musician will be prayerful—inviting God's leading and listening to God's direction. Pastoral leaders will be discerning; they will know their people and have a sensitivity to what is most appropriate (or not) within the context of the values suggested in the rubric. It is possible that a congregational song can earn high marks and yet not be appropriate for your own group of worshipers. It will be important for you to truly enter into the lives of your people so that the songs they sing not only meet high standards, but also express the experience and passion of your people.

In the end, worship leaders must have true spiritual wisdom. They will love God, love others, and be passionate about the worship of the church, all the while surrendering their own rights to sing the songs they may prefer, in favor of songs that glorify God in spirit and in truth.

It is our prayer and hope that this instrument will serve today's worship leaders well. We trust they will become more confident in their ability to choose strong worship songs. Those who select the songs their congregations sing exercise a great deal of power, for they influence the theology and the faith of their people for years to come.

# APPENDIX:

## THE WORSHIP SONG RUBRIC

| THE WORSHIP SONG RUBRIC: THEOLOGICAL CONSIDERATIONS | | | | |
|---|---|---|---|---|
| CATEGORY | 6 points | 4 points | 2 points | 0 points |
| Theological Integrity According to Song Type | **(A) PROCLAMATION** Expresses doctrinal essential/distinctive that:<br>• is faithful to Christian teachings that are central, nonnegotiable to Christianity or to a doctrinal distinctive of a given tradition;<br>• clearly and completely states the teaching;<br>• elaborates upon the teaching;<br>• expects worshiper to respond in specific ways (to praise, change, serve). | **(A) PROCLAMATION** Expresses doctrinal essential/distinctive that:<br>• is faithful to Christian teachings that are central, nonnegotiable to Christianity or to a doctrinal distinctive of a given tradition;<br>• is less clear and/or less completely stated;<br>• elaborates somewhat upon the teaching;<br>• suggests worshiper generally respond. | **(A) PROCLAMATION** Expresses doctrinal essential/distinctive that:<br>• is vague or questionable Christian teaching;<br>• is ambiguous and/or gives passing reference to stated teaching;<br>• offers little elaboration upon the teaching;<br>• may or may not expect worshiper to respond. | **(A) PROCLAMATION** Expresses doctrinal essential/distinctive that:<br>• is unfaithful to Christian teaching;<br>• fails to completely state the teaching;<br>• offers no real elaboration upon the teaching;<br>• expects no direct response from worshiper. |
| | **(B) PETITION** Voices prayerful petitions that:<br>• include sound theological instruction concerning prayer;<br>• are obviously consistent with biblical patterns of prayer. | **(B) PETITION** Voices prayerful petitions that:<br>• allude to theological precepts concerning prayer;<br>• are not inconsistent with biblical models of praying. | **(B) PETITION** Voices prayerful petitions that:<br>• suggest questionable teaching concerning prayer;<br>• suggest no biblical pattern of prayer. | **(B) PETITION** Voices prayerful petitions that:<br>• give false teaching concerning prayer;<br>• reflect a pattern that violates biblical models of praying. |
| | **(C) PRAISE** Expresses praise to God that:<br>• clearly states true aspects of God's nature and character;<br>• develops a deep understanding of God's nature and character;<br>• connects praise to the creative and saving actions of God;<br>• relates praise to the appropriate economies of the persons of the Godhead. | **(C) PRAISE** Expresses praise to God that:<br>• clearly states true aspects of God's nature and character;<br>• develops some understanding of God's nature and character;<br>• may or may not connect praise to the creative and saving actions of God;<br>• may or may not relate praise to the appropriate economies of the persons of the Godhead. | **(C) PRAISE** Expresses praise to God that:<br>• makes reference to God but without reference to God's nature/character;<br>• does not develop an understanding of God's nature and character;<br>• does not connect praise of God to action(s) of God;<br>• does not relate praise to the appropriate economies of the persons of the Godhead. | **(C) PRAISE** Expresses praise to God that:<br>• is generic and minimal in reference to God;<br>• lacks any theological development concerning God's nature/character;<br>• makes no connection to praise of God and action(s) of God;<br>• does not relate praise to the appropriate persons of the Godhead. |

(continued)

| THE WORSHIP SONG RUBRIC: THEOLOGICAL CONSIDERATIONS | | | |
|---|---|---|---|
| **CATEGORY** | **6 points** | **4 points** | **2 points** | **0 points** |
| **Theological Integrity According to Song Type** | **(D) EXHORTATION** Exhorts worshipers by: • focusing clearly and consistently upon encouragement or edification for the purposes of godliness and successful Christian living; • clearly reflecting the larger purposes of the kingdom rather than personal piety alone. | **(D) EXHORTATION** Exhorts worshipers by: • making an attempt to encourage or edify for the purposes of godliness and successful Christian living; (but) • failing to associate growth in godliness with the larger purposes of the kingdom. | **(D) EXHORTATION** Exhorts worshipers by: • offering vague or little encouragement or exhortation; (but) • failing to associate growth in godliness with the larger purposes of the kingdom. | **(D) EXHORTATION** Makes only a passing attempt to exhort by: • making little or no reference to the purpose for edification; (and) • failing to associate growth in godliness with the larger purposes of the kingdom. |
| | **(E) CALL TO ACTION** **Declares** an intention to respond to Word (and Sacrament) that: • declares explicitly what the singer will do; • clearly associates this intention with the need for divine grace or assistance; • clearly associates the intention with the larger purposes of the kingdom. | **(E) CALL TO ACTION** **Declares** an intention to respond to Word (and Sacrament) that: • declares generally what the singer will do; • indirectly associates this intention with the need for divine grace or assistance; • refers to the larger purposes of the kingdom. | **(E) CALL TO ACTION** **Invites or exhorts** a response to Word (and Sacrament) that: • suggests what worshipers should do; • offers vague or no need for divine grace or assistance; • suggests the larger purposes of the kingdom. | **(E) CALL TO ACTION** **Invites or exhorts** a response to Word (and Sacrament) that: • implies what worshipers could do; • violates a biblical essential or type of response, • does not refer to the larger purposes of the kingdom. |
| **Biblical Allusion and/or Story** | Song is rich in biblical language (biblical allusion, imagery, metaphor) and/or is detailed and complete in biblical narrative. | Song contains some biblical language and/or uses narrative in moderate detail and completeness. | Song uses little or no biblical language and/or attempts to use narrative but with little detail. | Song uses language, allusion, imagery, metaphor, or narrative that is opposing in nature to scriptural ideals. |
| **Trinitarian Ethos** | Recognizes and addresses the Triune nature of God by citing all three of the divine persons—Father, Son, and Holy Spirit—by name, title, or work. | Recognizes and addresses the Triune nature of God by citing one or more of the divine persons—Father, Son, and/or Holy Spirit—by name, title, or work. | Fails to recognize and address any divine person—Father, Son, or Holy Spirit—by name, title, or work. | Denies God's Triune nature by containing anti-Trinitarian thought. (For example, that Father, Son, and Spirit are the same person or that the three persons are separable in nature.) |
| **References to God** | Predominantly and consistently refers to or addresses God (or persons of God) by biblical names or titles. | Minimally refers to or addresses God (or persons of God) by biblical names or titles. | Makes no reference to biblical names or titles for God. | Uses names or titles for God that are inconsistent with biblical practice. |
| **Corporate Ethos** | Uses language for worshipers that explicitly indicates corporate assent/ understanding. | Uses language for worshipers that implicitly assumes a corporate assent/ understanding. | Uses language for worshipers that is a mixture of corporate and individual expression. | Uses language that is highly personal in expression. |

 (continued)

| THE WORSHIP SONG RUBRIC: LYRICAL CONSIDERATIONS | | | |
|---|---|---|---|
| **CATEGORY** | **3 points** | **2 points** | **1 points** | **0 points** |
| **Sentence Structures/ Grammar/Usage** | Lyrics include a variety of standard, well-chosen structures and consistently strong choices in grammar and usage. | Lyrics use standard and well-chosen structures and principles of grammar and usage. | Lyrics include instances of non-standard usage, awkward structures, or weak choices in grammar or usage. | Lyrics repeatedly include non-standard usage and/or awkward structures. |
| **Diction: Word Choice and Tone** | Lyrics show remarkable use of fresh or traditional language, good word choice, economy, and fully consistent tone. | Lyrics use fresh or appropriately traditional language, good word choice, economy, and consistency of tone. | Lyrics include instances of cliché, ineffective word choice, wordiness, and/or questionable tone. | Lyrics include frequent use of cliché, inappropriate word choice, wordiness, and/or inappropriate or potentially offensive tone. |
| **Coherence** | Lyrics show remarkable consistency and connections within and between themes and tone; remarkable connections within and among language, ideas, and images. | Lyrics show consistency within and between themes and tone; clear connections within and among language, ideas, and images. | Lyrics include instances of inconsistency in themes and tone; instances of failure to connect ideas and/or language. | Lyrics include frequent inconsistencies in themes and tone; repeated failure to connect ideas and/or language. |
| **Euphony/Sound** | Lyrics show remarkable grace and remarkable or surprising use of rhyme and other sound devices. | Lyrics show general grace and effective rhyme and other sound devices. | Lyrics include instances of gracelessness, including difficult-to-articulate words or phrases, flat or awkward sounds, predictable rhyme, and/or ineffective sound devices. | Lyrics include repeated, difficult-to-articulate words and phrases, forced rhyme, repeated awkward sounds, and/or pervasive, ineffective use of sound devices. |
| **Figurative Language** | Lyrics show remarkable, artful use of figurative language, imagery, and specificity. | Lyrics use imagery and figurative language well; generalization or abstraction is tempered by image or specificity. | Lyrics include instances of cliché, stale imagery or figurative language, or excessive use of generalization or abstraction. | Lyrics are clichéd, use inappropriate figurative language (such as mixed metaphor) and/or pervasive generalization or abstraction. |

                    (continued)

| THE WORSHIP SONG RUBRIC: MUSICAL CONSIDERATIONS | | | | |
|---|---|---|---|---|
| **CATEGORY** | **3 points** | **2 points** | **1 points** | **0 points** |
| **Melody** | Melody has direction, uses leaps and steps judiciously, is balanced in vocal range, uses standard melodic features, stands on its own, and is memorable. | Melody has moderate direction, uses a few awkward leaps and steps, rests heavily in one part of the range, and/or is somewhat memorable. | Melody lacks direction, treats leaps and steps awkwardly, is somewhat monotonous, or is not easily remembered. | Melody lacks logic, variety, appeal, and is not memorable. |
| **Rhythmic Vitality** | Rhythm has direction, is interesting, portrays the action of the text, assists in good declamation, and is reasonable for the singers to master. | Rhythm is of moderate interest; does not add to or detract from the melody and/or text, or has one or more obstacles for the singers. | Rhythm is unnecessarily repetitious, draws attention to itself, is inconsistent in the use of accents with the text, and/or discourages the singers. | Rhythm works against the melody and/or text, defeating the message of the song, or is too difficult to sing. |
| **Harmonic Support** | Harmony facilitates the progression of the melody, enriches the melody without covering it, uses helpful amounts of dissonance and consonance, and/or lends itself to singing in parts | Harmony is somewhat predictable, use of dissonance and/or consonance is questionable, and/or lends itself less to singing in parts. | Harmony is dull and predictable. | Harmony is in conflict with the melody and text. |
| **Compatibility of Music and Text** | Musical components contribute significantly in supporting, highlighting, and interpreting the text. | Some but not all of the musical components contribute to the text. | Musical components neither contribute to nor detract from the text; compatibility is neutral. | Some musical components seem to be in conflict with the tenor of the text. |
| **Suitability for Singing** | Music is accessible for corporate singing in relation to vocal range, structural repetition, and ease of unison and/or singing in parts. | Music includes some hindrances to corporate singing. | Music has significant hindrances to corporate singing in one or more aspects. | Music is too difficult to sing corporately. |

# GLOSSARY

**Biblical allusion:** A biblical allusion is a figure of speech that makes direct or indirect reference to a biblical person, event, or teaching.

**Call to action:** A call to action is a call to a specific response to God's Word in proclamation and/or sacrament by an individual or congregation.

**Cliché:** An expression or idea which has been overused to the point of losing its effectiveness.

**Coherence:** A sense of unity often created by purposeful arrangement, parallelism, repetition, or thematic consistency.

**Complex sentence:** A sentence with at least one independent clause and at least one subordinate clause.

**Compound sentence:** A sentence with two or more independent clauses.

**Consonance:** Combining pitches so as to relieve tension; nonconflicting sounds as perceived by the listener.

**Declamation:** The coinciding of the verbal accent with the musical accent.

**Diction:** Choice of words, their arrangement, and the force, accuracy, and grace with which they are used.

**Dissonance:** Combining pitches so as to create tension; conflicting sounds as perceived by the listener.

**Doctrinal differences:** Doctrinal differences are important Christian doctrines with which there can be some latitude in belief. While important, having implications for worship and practice, they are negotiable in Christianity.

**Doctrinal essential:** A doctrinal essential is a nonnegotiable of Christianity. Essentials represent the core ideas of Christianity without which Christianity ceases being Christian.

**Doctrine:** Christian doctrine is specific Christian teaching on any theological topic.

**End rhyme:** Rhyme that occurs in the last syllables of lines of poetry.

**Euphony:** The acoustic effect produced by words combined to please the ear.

**Exhortation:** Encouragement or edification of the individual Christian or church.

**Figurative language:** Language that goes beyond the literal meaning of words in order to furnish new effects or fresh insights into an idea or a subject. The most common figures of speech are simile, metaphor, and alliteration.

**God's character:** God's character refers to God's moral attributes—God's holiness, justice, righteousness, goodness, and love.

**God's nature:** God's nature addresses the substance, essence, or being of God. This is a philosophical term related to God's ontology—the "substance" that the Father, Son, and Holy Spirit share making them one God. While we can know attributes of God's nature, God's nature is completely unknowable to us.

**Grammar:** The set of principles that govern the structure and composition of sentences, phrases, and words. It is sometimes referred to as *syntax*.

**Harmony:** Notes composed for additional voices or instruments to complement, adorn, or dialogue with the melody.

**Imagery:** Language that appeals to one or more of your five senses (hearing, taste, touch, smell, sight).

**Lyrics:** The set of words in a song.

**Melody:** The arrangement of musical notes that constitute a recognizable and memorable tune.

**Metaphor:** A comparison between two dissimilar things intending to illuminate one important similarity between the two.

**Narrative:** A narrative is a story. The Bible as a whole is a narrative of God, creation, fall, redemption, and consummation. This is the Christian narrative.

**Off rhyme/slant rhyme:** Rhyme in which there is close but not exact correspondence of sounds (as in *made/bed* or *holy/hollow*).

**Parallelism:** Similarity of structure in a pair or series of related words, phrases, or clauses.

**Petition:** Generally, petition refers to the work of prayer. More specifically, it refers to the prayer on behalf of others and ourselves.

**Praise:** Praise is the exaltation of God for who God is and for what God has done.

**Proclamation:** Proclamation is the communication of the Word of God and sound Christian doctrine.

**Range:** The distance between the lowest and highest notes in a melody.

**Rhythm:** The assigning of note values (longer/shorter) and accents to create a recognizable pattern of pulses; aids in moving the melody forward in time.

**Song:** A musical entity consisting of two basic elements: melody and words.

**Theology:** Theology is a broad term addressing all areas related to the study of God and statements on God.

**Tone:**  The emotional coloring of an artistic work.

**Trinitarian ethos:** At the heart of Christianity is the revelation of God as Triune, one God in three divine persons. A Trinitarian ethos recognizes this central truth of Christianity and is intentional in incorporating this distinctly Christian understanding of God in worship.

**Trinity:** Historic Christianity teaches that there is one God in three co-equal persons—Father, Son, and Holy Spirit. The Father is God, the Son is God, and the Spirit is God. However, the Father is distinguishable from the Son, and the Son is distinguishable from the Spirit. Each divine person has all that properly belongs to the divine nature: eternality, omnipotence, wisdom, goodness, holiness, love, as well as other divine attributes. The persons of the Trinity can be distinguished but not separated. Their distinction is not in nature, for they share one divine nature without separation into parts; rather, their distinction is in relationship with one another: the Father begets the Son and the Father with the Son breathes the Holy Spirit.  They are one in nature, three in persons.

**Tune:**  The melody of a composition.

**Usage:**  The customary, accepted way in which a language or a form of a language is spoken or written among native speakers.